Baptist Identity Series
PERSONAL STUDY GUIDES

William M. Pinson, Jr.
Doris A. Tinker
with
Dennis A. Parrott ~ Skyler G. Tinker

Baptist Identity Series
PERSONAL STUDY GUIDES

Baptist Identity Series
A resource from the Texas Baptist Heritage Center
William M. Pinson, Jr., Director
Doris A. Tinker, Director of Communications/Organization

Printed in the United States of America

First Edition: 2014
ISBN-13: 978-1-934741-22-1
ISBN-10:   1-934741-22-1

Table of Contents

Baptist Identity Series: A Word of Introduction 4

Suggestions on How to Use the Personal Study Guides 5

Personal Study Guides:

   1. Baptists: Who? Where? What? Why? 7

   2. Baptists: What Makes a Baptist a Baptist? 11

   3. Jesus Is Lord 15

   4. The Authority of the Bible 19

   5. Is Soul Competency *THE* Baptist Distinctive? 23

   6. Baptists: Salvation By Grace Through Faith Alone 27

   7. Baptists: The Priesthood of the *Believer* or of *Believers?* 31

   8. Baptists: Believer's Baptism 35

   9. Baptists Believe in a Regenerate Church Membership 39

  10. Congregational Church Governance 43

  11. Baptist Autonomy: Difficulties and Benefits 47

  12. Baptist Church Life: Organization, Officers, Worship, Ordinances 51

  13. Baptists and Voluntary Cooperation 55

  14. Baptists and Evangelism 59

  15. Baptists and Missions 63

  16. Baptists and Ministry 67

  17. Baptists and Christian Education 71

  18. Baptists: Applying the Gospel 75

  19. Baptists: Champions of Religious Freedom 79

Answers to the Fill in the Blanks 83

About the *Baptist Identity Series* 86

Contributors to the *Baptist Identity Series* 87

How to Order Materials in the *Baptist Identity Series* 88

Baptist Identity Series:
A Word of Introduction

This book is a companion to the nineteen topical leaflets in the *Baptist Identity Series*. It provides guides for persons to study the material in the leaflets. We the authors of the *Baptist Identity Series* pray that your study will be a blessing not only to you personally but also to the cause of Christ.

As you begin your study of the *Baptist Identity Series*, it will be helpful to know why these nineteen topics were selected and the approach taken. Some other Christian groups also treasure many of the beliefs that Baptists hold dear, but taken as a whole the beliefs and practices set forth in the nineteen leaflets set Baptists apart as a distinctive member of the Christian family. Being distinctive does not necessarily mean better, of course, but it does indicate a difference.

The beliefs that are shared with other Christian denominations, such as doctrines related to God, are dealt with throughout the leaflets and study guides rather than separately. This is done to highlight the fact that beliefs and practices distinctive to Baptists are rooted in these basic doctrines.

The leaflets are designed to handle each topic in both a concise way and in a general fashion. The *Series* does not attempt to present an in-depth study of the various interpretations held by Baptists but rather to indicate how Baptists in general view the topics. A statement in the leaflets to the effect that Baptists believe or do certain things does not necessarily indicate that Baptists are the only ones who believe or act in that way; persons in other denominations may also hold these beliefs.

The leaflets contain key scriptures on each topic. In addition each guide in the *Personal Study Guides* book lists a scripture passage for memorization. The printed scripture passages are from the King James Version of the Bible unless indicated to be from the New International Version (NIV) of the Bible. Those from the NIV are from the edition published by the International Bible Society copyrighted 1973, 1978, 1984. Since the approach taken in the *Series* is biblical, you will find it very helpful to have a Bible handy as you study.

Hopefully, the *Series* will encourage you to further your studies and consult other materials on the various topics. The website www.baptistdistinctives.org is designed to assist in additional study.

Suggestions on How to Use the Personal Study Guides

This book of personal study guides is designed for use by persons either in individual or group study on the topics in the nineteen Baptist Identity Leaflets. The leaflets are in the book *Baptist Beliefs and Heritage,* an 11 x 8.5 book which also contains a summary of Baptist history, biographical sketches of Baptist leaders, insights on key words and terms used in the materials, historical vignettes, and brief accounts of persons and events in Baptist heritage. The leaflets are also available as nineteen separate leaflets in a 4-page 5.5 x 8.5 format. *Leader's Guide for Group Study,* a book for leaders of groups studying the nineteen leaflets, is also available.

Each of the study guides in this book is divided into five sections: (1) a scripture for memory, (2) a fill-in-the-blanks activity based on the related leaflet, (3) a series of questions for application, (4) an encouragement to apply the scriptures related to the topic, along with suggestions for scripture memory, and (5) suggestions for prayer.

For each of these studies you will need a copy of the leaflet on that topic, a Bible, and a pen or pencil. If you do not already have copies of the leaflets, please see the How to Order Materials section in this book.

The following are possible uses for the leaflets and personal study guides:

Topical Study. For each leaflet's topic, read the leaflet and do the activities in the related personal study guide.

Personal Bible Study. Read the leaflet and the related scriptures, including both the scriptures printed in the leaflet and the scriptures that are referenced but not printed in the leaflet. After reading the leaflet and the related Bible passages, do the activities in the study guide.

Personal Devotional Time. Read the leaflet and utilize the suggestions for prayer in the study guide. The section on prayer fits well into a time of personal devotionals.

Family Worship Time. Each leaflet and its related study guide can be adapted to family worship where applicable. The family worship time could include reading the scriptures printed in the leaflet, discussing some of the application questions in the study guide, and utilizing the suggestions in the prayer section.

Sharing with Others. Share a set of the leaflets and the book of personal study guides with others.

We pray that as you use this
workbook in your study of the
Baptist Identity Leaflets that it
will contribute to your understanding
of Baptist belief and heritage.

Baptists
Who? Where? What? Why?

The following activities are based on the Baptist Identity Leaflet No. 1.

Scripture Memory

"Yea, I have a goodly heritage." Psalm 16:6

Fill in the Blanks

1. Little is known about Baptists by the world in general and what is known is often _____.

2. Some Baptists are not familiar with Baptist _____ and _____, _____, and _____.

3. Diverse in many ways, Baptists are defined, not by a single doctrine, but by a _____ ____ _____ _____ _____.

4. In what ways are Baptists diverse?

      a. _____

      b. _____

      c. _____

      d. _____

      e. _____

      f. _____

5. Baptists live, worship, and minister in more than a _____ _____.

6. It is estimated that approximately ____ _____ baptized believers are members of Baptist churches worldwide.

7. The largest concentration of Baptists is in _____ _____.

8. The slowest growth among Baptists in the world is in _____ and _____ _____.

9. Through _____ and _____ Baptists have helped to transform the lives of millions of people.

10. Baptists minister to a plethora of _____ _____.

11. Basic Baptist doctrines include: the _____ of Christ, the _____ as the sole written authority for faith and practice, _____ _____, salvation by a _____ response of repentance and faith, the _____ of all believers, baptism only of _____ and only by _____, and a _____ voluntary church membership.

12. Basic Baptist polities include: Congregational _____ _____, the _____ of Baptist churches and other Baptist entities, _____ and the _____ _____ as symbolic, financial support by _____ and _____, and _____ _____ freely chosen under the Lordship of Christ.

13. Basic Baptist practices include: _____, _____, _____, the application of the _____ to all of life, and _____ _____.

14. _____, never coercion, permeates these convictions.

15. Baptists differ in many ways, but they generally concur on _____ _____ and _____.

Application Questions

1. Is the impression of Baptists in your community basically favorable or unfavorable? On what do you base your opinion? Why do you believe people have this impression?

2. Is there any hesitancy on your part to let your friends and acquaintances know that you are a Baptist, if you are? Why or why not?

3. What are some of the reasons why it is good that Baptists are very diverse?

4. Why do you think that the greatest growth among Baptists at the end of the twentieth century was taking place outside North America?

5. What do you consider to be the greatest contribution of Baptists to the world? Why?

6. In what ways are you enjoying the religious freedom that is precious to Baptists?

7. Which of the basic beliefs of Baptists seems most important, and why do you feel this way?

8. Which of the basic Baptist polities seems most important, and why do you feel this way?

9. Which of the basic Baptist practices mentioned in the leaflet seems most important to you and why?

Scripture Application and Memory

Read the scripture in the Scripture Memory section, prayerfully consider how it applies to you, and memorize the passage and its reference.

> Scripture memory suggestion: **Read** the scripture and reference aloud. **Record** the scripture and reference in your own handwriting. **Review** the scripture word by word. **Reflect** about the meaning and the message it has for you personally. **Recall** the scripture and reference from memory throughout your study time without looking at the scripture.

Suggestions for Prayer

1. Pray for thoughtful boldness in sharing Christ with others.

2. Pray for Baptists as they minister throughout the world, especially for those in dangerous situations.

3. Thank God for living in a country where there is freedom of religion to worship God according to the dictates of one's conscience.

4. Pray for your church that it will be true to the teachings of the Bible in its beliefs, polity, and practices.

STUDY NOTES

For additional study resources, see www.baptistdistinctives.org

Baptists
What Makes a Baptist a Baptist?

The following activities are based on the Baptist Identity Leaflet No. 2.

Scripture Memory

"...Always be prepared to give an answer to everyone who asks you to give the reason for the hope that you have. But do this with gentleness and respect..." 1 Peter 3:15 (NIV)

Fill in the Blanks

1. Sometimes people do not distinguish between a _____ and a _____ _____.

2. "Denomination" describes a set of _____ and _____ held in common by a group of persons.

3. Denominations usually develop various _____ to help fulfill the values and beliefs of the denomination.

4. Some of the factors that have resulted in different denominations include: the nature of the _____, the way of _____, and the meaning of _____.

5. Denominations are important because they make a big difference in the lives of _____ and in the _____.

6. True or false? There is no single belief or practice that makes Baptists distinctive from other Christians.   _____

7. A combination of _____ and _____ sets Baptists apart from other denominations.

8. While Baptists differ on a number of issues, _____ _____ must be included for the recipe to produce a Baptist.

9. One of the greatest contributors to a lack of knowledge about Baptists in Baptist churches is the increasing number of people joining from _____ _____.

10. True or false? There is a growing interest in Baptist beliefs.
_____

11. Who said, "Every Baptist ought to know why he is a Baptist, and to know it from the specific commands of God's Word"?
_____ ___ _____

12. There are _____ _____ which we hold dear as Baptists that are compelling reasons to be part of the _____
_____.

13. The _____ _____ has made and continues to make a difference in the world.

Note: The fill in the blanks on numbers 14, 15, 16, 17 relate to the box in the leaflet entitled "The Baptist Recipe."

14. Some beliefs such as _____ ____ _____ and in _____ _____ as Savior are found in most Christian denominations.

15. Two major differences between Baptists and most Christian denominations include: a different view of _____, the Baptist denomination has no _____ _____.

16. The common ingredient in all of the organizations of the Baptist denomination is _____ _____.

17. The desire of Baptists is to be as close to the _____ _____ model for an individual Christian and for a church as is humanly possible with God's help through the instruction and empowering of the Holy Spirit.

Application Questions

1. Why is there no single belief or practice that defines who Baptists are but rather there is a group of beliefs and practices that defines Baptists?

2. Which, if any, of these basic beliefs or doctrines are you not familiar with?

3. Which, if any, of these basic beliefs or doctrines would you find difficult to explain to a non-Baptist?

4. In what ways is the form of governance followed by your church in keeping with the basic Baptist polity of congregational (that is member) rule of a church?

5. What are some of the reasons for your church to cooperate with an association of churches, a state or regional Baptist organization, and a national Baptist organization?

6. Since the Bible is to be the authoritative guide for the beliefs and practices of a Baptist church, why are there different kinds of Baptist churches in matters such as worship styles, the titles of church officers or leaders, or relation to other churches?

7. What are the main reasons that caused you to join your church?

8. What are some of the reasons why it is important for all of the members of a church to understand basic Baptist beliefs and doctrines?

9. Which of the ministries of your church are most important to you and why?

Scripture Application and Memory

Read the scripture in the Scripture Memory section, prayerfully consider how it applies to you, and memorize the passage and its reference.

> Scripture memory suggestion: **Read** the scripture and reference aloud. **Record** the scripture and reference in your own handwriting. **Review** the scripture word by word. **Reflect** about the meaning and the message it has for you personally. **Recall** the scripture and reference from memory throughout your study time without looking at the scripture.

Suggestions for Prayer

1. Thank God for the Baptist Christians of past generations who diligently sought to base their beliefs and practices on the Bible.

2. Thank God for the number of faithful Baptist Christians who through centuries remained true to their understanding of the Bible's teachings in spite of persecution and ridicule.

3. Pray for Baptists and other Christians throughout the world who suffer persecution for their beliefs.

4. Pray that the current generation of Baptist Christians will remain true to the beliefs and practices based on the Bible.

5. Pray that Baptist individuals will be faithful in sharing the gospel and ministering to persons in Jesus' name.

STUDY NOTES

For additional study resources, see www.baptistdistinctives.org

Jesus Is Lord

The following activities are based on the Baptist Identity Leaflet No. 3.

Scripture Memory

"...every tongue should confess that Jesus Christ is Lord, to the glory of God the Father." Philippians 2:11

Fill in the Blanks

Note: The fill in the blanks on numbers 3, 4, 5, 6 relate to the box on the first page of the leaflet: "The Importance of the Baptist Commitment to the Lordship of Christ."

1. As Christians we confess that Jesus Christ is Lord because we owe him our
_____ _____, _____ _____, and
_____ _____ because of who he _____ and what
he has _____.

2. The Bible gives a number of reasons why Jesus is Lord of all including that
he is _____, he _____ on the cross, he _____ from the dead,
and he _____ into heaven.

3. The Bible teaches _____ _____ ____ _____, and
Baptists look to the _____ as their sole written authority.

4. The biblical teaching about _____ _____ demands
that each individual Christian bow to no ultimate authority other than _____.

5. The biblical emphasis on soul competency flows from _____
_____ ____ _____.

6. Christ, alone, is _____ _____ ____ _____ _____.

7. The Bible sets forth the extent of Christ's Lordship; for example Jesus is
Lord of all _____, of every _____, and of _____.

8. The Bible teaches that Christ's Lordship is _____.

9. Persons are not puppets; their Creator has given them _____ and _____ ____ _____.

10. Baptists insist that each person has the God-given _____ and _____ to find and follow the will of Jesus as Lord.

11. The Lordship of Christ means that persons and churches ought to be free from coercion by _____ or _____ _____ in spiritual and religious matters.

12. Thomas Helwys wrote a book in protest of _____ _____, who set himself up as the head of the church.

13. For individual Christians and for the churches of which they are part to be under the Lordship of Christ means that they should acknowledge Christ as _____, recognize responsibility to make decisions regarding the church under the Lordship of Christ, and realize that _____ of the members of a church are responsible for decisions regarding it.

14. The Lordship of Christ is a basic _____ _____.

Application Questions

1. What does the Lordship of Christ mean to you personally?

2. What are some ways that your church could be tempted to allow something or someone other than Jesus Christ to be the Lord of the church?

3. What are some ways that you can celebrate the four reasons given in the leaflet for declaring Jesus to be Lord of all?

4. What new understanding, if any, have you gained from reading the leaflet regarding the importance of soul competency?

5. Have you or someone you know experienced any type of suffering because of a stand taken regarding religious liberty?

6. What are some examples of how church members may try to usurp Christ's role as head of the church?

7. What could be done in your church to help ensure that every decision is made in such a way to reflect that Christ is the Lord of the church?

8. Since the Lordship of Christ is a basic doctrine for all Christians, in what way does the Baptist emphasis on the Lordship of Christ seem to be different from some other Christian denominations?

9. In what ways is your church governance a demonstration of the Lordship of Christ over the church and individual members?

Scripture Application and Memory

Read the scriptures referenced in the leaflet and prayerfully consider how they apply to you. Memorize the passage and its reference in the Scripture Memory section.

> Scripture memory suggestion: **Read** the scripture and reference aloud. **Record** the scripture and reference in your own handwriting. **Review** the scripture word by word. **Reflect** about the meaning and the message it has for you personally. **Recall** the scripture and reference from memory throughout your study time without looking at the scripture.

Suggestions for Prayer

1. Pray that Christ will indeed be the Lord of your life in every way.

2. Pray that your church will demonstrate in every way, such as governance, worship, and ministry, that Christ is Lord of the church.

3. Thank God for the religious freedom that we enjoy in our nation to live under the Lordship of Christ without the severe persecution that persons have endured in the past and that many still endure in other places.

4. Pray for all persons to acknowledge that Jesus Christ is Lord.

STUDY NOTES

For additional study resources, see www.baptistdistinctives.org

The Authority of the Bible

The following activities are based on the Baptist Identity Leaflet No. 4.

Scripture Memory

"All Scripture is God-breathed and is useful for teaching, rebuking, correcting and training in righteousness, so that the man of God may be thoroughly equipped for every good work." 2 Timothy 3:16-17 (NIV)

Fill in the Blanks

1. The scripture 2 Timothy 3:16-17 reminds us that Baptists have considered the Bible as authoritative for faith and practice because of its very _____.

2. The Bible stands alone among all other writings in that it is _____ _____ _____ and about _____.

3. If proof is needed of the divine, authoritative nature of the Bible, consider the following:

     a. The amazing _____ of the Bible.

     b. The fulfillment of _____ _____ _____.

     c. The continuing _____ of the Bible's message.

     d. The _____ of its message to _____ lives and society.

     e. The repeated _____ within the Bible to be the Word of God.

4. Baptists may gain insight from other documents or teachers but they refuse to accept them as _____.

5. Baptists do not worship the _____ but rather they worship the _____ of the Bible.

6. The Bible is our sole _____ authority and God is our
_____ authority.

7. The Bible becomes for us a _____ of God.

8. The _____ of Christ and the _____ of the Bible
go hand in hand.

9. The Holy Spirit _____ or _____ persons to
interpret and apply the Bible.

10. "The Bible is primarily a book of _____," stated Herschel Hobbs
in *The Baptist Faith and Message.*

11. The Bible is foundational for _____ _____ and
_____ _____.

12. Baptists declare that all people should have the freedom to
_____, _____, and _____ the Bible for themselves.

13. Guidelines for ensuring correct interpretations as we study the Bible
include the following:

    a. Study the Bible prayerfully and humbly depending on
_____ from the Holy Spirit.

    b. Share interpretations with a fellowship of _____.

    c. Use sound _____ of interpretation.

    d. Make comparisons with the interpretations of _____
_____, past and present.

14. Although Baptists may disagree about what the Bible teaches on certain
subjects, Baptists agree that the _____ is the _____ _____
_____ _____ for faith and practice.

Application Questions

1. Why have Baptists through the years been willing to risk their lives for their conviction that the Bible is the sole written authority for faith and practice?

2. What proof regarding the authority of the Bible is most important to you?

3. Have you ever been tempted to accept a creed or some other human authority other than the authority of the Bible in your life or in the life of your church? If so, what?

4. What should be our ultimate response to the authority of the Bible?

5. What argument could be offered for or against the Bible being included as a required textbook in our public schools?

6. How do you balance your personal study and interpretation of the Bible with what other interpreters have to say?

7. What is the danger of individual believers studying and interpreting the Bible for themselves? What is a greater danger?

8. What are some of the important beliefs that Baptists base on the authority of the Bible?

9. What reasons could you give for why the Bible is not just another religious book?

Scripture Application and Memory

Read the scripture in the Scripture Memory section, prayerfully consider how it applies to you, and memorize the passage and its reference.

> Scripture memory suggestion: **Read** the scripture and reference aloud. **Record** the scripture and reference in your own handwriting. **Review** the scripture word by word. **Reflect** about the meaning and the message it has for you personally. **Recall** the scripture and reference from memory throughout your study time without looking at the scripture.

Suggestions for Prayer

1. Pray for persons throughout the world to have access to a Bible and freedom to read, interpret, and apply it to life.

2. Thank God for the gift of the Bible and its message of salvation.

3. Pray for God's guidance through the Holy Spirit in understanding and applying the teachings of the Bible.

4. Pray that you will consistently, regularly, and carefully study the Bible.

STUDY NOTES

For additional study resources, see www.baptistdistinctives.org

Is Soul Competency
THE Baptist Distinctive?

The following activities are based on the Baptist Identity Leaflet No. 5.

Scripture Memory

"Choose you this day whom ye will serve." Joshua 24:15

Fill in the Blanks

1. Baptists emphasize that soul competency is not a mere human characteristic, but a _____ _____ _____.

2. In creation God gave to persons the freedom ____ _____ _____.

3. The Bible is filled with examples of _____ _____.

4. For example, the _____ _____ assume the competency of human beings to understand them and the freedom to accept or to reject them.

5. The people of Israel were given _____, indicating a competency ____ _____ _____.

6. The heroes of the faith in the Old Testament, such as _____, _____, and _____, refused to give up their freedom of conscience to government rulers.

7. Jesus never _____ persons to follow him.

8. Jesus never violated the _____ _____ of individuals.

9. _____ _____ in the New Testament modeled soul competency.

10. Some people choose to attack the idea of soul competency contending that such freedom would limit _____ _____.

11. Others oppose the belief in soul competency because they claim it leads to _____ _____ and _____.

12. Still others accuse the concept of soul competency of resulting in _____ and hyper-individualism.

13. Although soul competency may not be *the* Baptist distinctive, it is certainly _____ to all other Baptist beliefs.

14. For example, soul competency relates to Baptist beliefs such as the _____ of the _____, _____ by grace through faith, _____ _____, _____ of all believers and _____ _____.

15. One of the reasons why both secular and religious despots have persecuted Baptists is that these persons _____ _____.

16. Baptists will do well to always emphasize that freedom carries _____.

Application Questions

1. Why is it important to you to be able to maintain the God-given freedom to relate to God directly?

2. What aspect of the concept of soul competency means the most to you?

3. What examples can you think of in history or current events where people are trying to deny freedom of choice?

4. In what way should our beliefs about soul competency affect our approach to evangelism?

5. Does a better understanding of soul competency on your part lead you to feelings of arrogance or of humility? What is the reason for your answer?

6. In what way is a belief in soul competency related to other basic Baptist beliefs founded on the teachings of the Bible?

7. How is the belief in soul competency closely related to the belief in the priesthood of all believers?

8. Why do you think that Herschel Hobbs wrote about soul competency that "out of this principle flow all other elements of Baptist belief...."?

Scripture Application and Memory

Read the scriptures referenced in the leaflet and prayerfully consider how they apply to you. Memorize the passage and its reference in the Scripture Memory section.

> Scripture memory suggestion: **Read** the scripture and reference aloud. **Record** the scripture and reference in your own handwriting. **Review** the scripture word by word. **Reflect** about the meaning and the message it has for you personally. **Recall** the scripture and reference from memory throughout your study time without looking at the scripture.

Suggestions for Prayer

1. Pray thanking God for the gift of "the principle of the competency of the soul in religion under God," as E. Y. Mullins expressed it.

2. Pray for courage to exercise this God-given competence in spite of challenges and obstacles.

3. Thank God for giving to early Baptists the fortitude to exercise their soul competency in spite of persecution by both government and religious authorities.

4. Pray for a deep desire to exercise your soul competency by prayerfully seeking to find and follow God's will.

STUDY NOTES

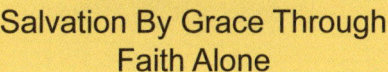

Baptists:

Salvation By Grace Through Faith Alone

The following activities are based on the Baptist Identity Leaflet No. 6.

Scripture Memory

"For by grace are ye saved through faith; and that not of yourselves: it is the gift of God: Not of works, lest any man should boast." Ephesians 2:8-9

Fill in the Blanks

1. The Bible clearly teaches that all have _____ and that the penalty for sin is _____ _____.

2. God by his grace has provided a way for _____ to be forgiven, _____ avoided, and _____ gained. That way is _____ in his Son, Jesus Christ.

3. Salvation, according to the Bible, is solely by _____ and _____, not by human effort or _____.

4. Since a man or woman cannot save himself or herself, God, out of love for humankind, has provided _____.

5. God's gift of salvation is available through _____ in his Son, the Lord Jesus Christ.

6. Some denominations have included such things as _____, _____ _____, _____ _____ or _____ as necessary for salvation.

7. Baptists have insisted that salvation comes only by _____ in God's _____ _____ of Jesus.

8. While Baptists insist that salvation is free, a gift from God, they also proclaim its _____.

9. Salvation ought never to be considered _____.

10. Practically all Baptist statements of belief emphasize that the Bible reveals that salvation includes _____,
_____, and _____.

11. _____ _____ do not result in salvation, but salvation is to result in _____ _____.

12. Baptists believe that true faith can never be _____.

13. Baptists note that Jesus never _____ anyone to follow him.

14. Baptists have consistently advocated _____ ____
_____, that is, religious freedom.

15. Not all Baptists have agreed on the _____ of God's sovereignty and humankind's _____ _____.

16. Most Baptists believe that the Bible sets forth both God's _____ and humankind's _____ ____
_____.

17. Baptists insist that anyone who responds through _____
_____ _____ in Jesus' atoning life, death, and resurrection can be
_____.

18. Most Baptists also believe that once a person has been truly saved, he or she is kept by the power of God; this is often termed _____
____ ____ _____.

Application Questions

1. What are some of the different ideas that you have heard about how persons get to heaven?

2. How would you explain the concept of sin and the need for forgiveness to someone who is not a Christian?

3. What should be the appropriate response to someone who advocates a works-based religion?

4. In what ways would you explain the "dynamic" nature of salvation, perhaps using words other than those often found in doctrinal statements, such as regeneration, sanctification, and glorification?

5. In what ways do you relate the sovereignty of God, that is God being all-knowing and all-powerful, to the freedom and responsibility of persons to make choices?

6. How do you respond to persons who think that Baptists are too narrow-minded regarding salvation?

7. Have you made a personal faith commitment to Jesus Christ as Lord and Savior? How can you encourage others to make such a commitment?

8. Why do you think that many people want to add something to faith in regard to salvation, such as baptism, good works, or church membership?

Scripture Application and Memory

Read the scriptures referenced in the leaflet and prayerfully consider how they apply to you. Memorize the passage and its reference in the Scripture Memory section.

> Scripture memory suggestion: **Read** the scripture and reference aloud. **Record** the scripture and reference in your own handwriting. **Review** the scripture word by word. **Reflect** about the meaning and the message it has for you personally. **Recall** the scripture and reference from memory throughout your study time without looking at the scripture.

Suggestions for Prayer

1. Thank God for his gift of salvation through faith in Jesus Christ.

2. Pray thanking God for the life that you enjoy in Christ, if you have indeed believed in him as your personal Lord and Savior.

3. Pray that your church will faithfully share the message of salvation throughout all of its various ministries and programs.

4. Pray for opportunities to share the good news about God's Son.

STUDY NOTES

Baptists:
The Priesthood of the *Believer*
or of *Believers?*

The following activities are based on the Baptist Identity Leaflet No. 7.

Scripture Memory

"Ye are a chosen generation, a royal priesthood, a holy nation, a peculiar people; that ye should shew forth the praises of him who hath called you out of darkness into his marvelous light." 1 Peter 2:9

Fill in the Blnks

1. Baptists insist that all who believe in Jesus as Lord and Savior are
_____, _____ _____.

2. Being a priest involves both _____ and _____.

3. The _____ _____ played an important role in the Old Testament but with the life, death, and resurrection of Jesus this changed because Jesus gave himself as a sacrifice for sin—a "once and for all act."

4. All who believe in Jesus become _____ with direct access to God, making _____ _____ no longer needed.

5. A believer priest has a responsibility to _____ his or her knowledge of God with other persons in _____ and _____.

6. This responsibility is carried out in various ways by Baptists, such as in
_____, _____, _____, and _____ _____ to benefit others.

7. _____ _____, a leader in the Protestant Reformation, is often linked with the concept of the priesthood of believers.

8. Martin Luther did not call for the elimination of the role of _____ but indicated that all persons had a priestly function.

9. The concept of the priesthood of believers is primarily based on the
_____ _____.

10. The priesthood of each believer is tied closely to the Baptist concept of
_____ _____.

11. Individuals can and should _____ and _____ the _____ for themselves under the guidance of the Holy Spirit.

12. There is only one High Priest, _____ _____.

13. A local church has many believer _____ as members who are to communicate the love and forgiveness of God.

14. The New Testament also speaks of the priesthood of _____.

15. Being a Christian involves _____ with other believers.

16. The competent and wise believer will seek insight and understanding from other _____ _____.

17. The Baptist model of a _____ rests on the concept of the priesthood of believers.

18. The will of the High Priest, Jesus Christ, is sought through _____, _____ _____, _____, and _____.

19. The term _____ _____ ____ _____ _____ communicates the biblical emphasis on the individual and soul competency. The term _____ ____ _____ communicates the biblical emphasis on community and fellowship.

20. Throughout history a tension has existed between the _____ and the _____.

Application Questions

1. Which responsibility of priesthood gives you the greatest concern? Why?

2. What would be your response to persons whose religions have a special priestly class who want to know why Baptists don't?

3. How can your church help you do a better job of sharing with others in word and action?

4. How would you rate the effectiveness of the fellowship aspect of your church?

5. What is your definition of "church"?

6. What do you believe the primary functions of a church should be? On what do you base this belief?

7. How can the balance between the individual believer and the group of believers be achieved or maintained in your church?

8. What is the difference between the "priesthood of the believer" and the "priesthood of believers"? How are these two concepts related?

9. How is the priesthood of all believers related to the concept of soul competency that is precious to Baptists?

10. Are there any changes you will make in your life as a Christian because of deeper insights into the concept of the priesthood of the believer?

Scripture Application and Memory

Read the scriptures referenced in the leaflet and prayerfully consider how they apply to you. Memorize the passage and its reference in the Scripture Memory section.

> Scripture memory suggestion: **Read** the scripture and reference aloud. **Record** the scripture and reference in your own handwriting. **Review** the scripture word by word. **Reflect** about the meaning and the message it has for you personally. **Recall** the scripture and reference from memory throughout your study time without looking at the scripture.

Suggestions for Prayer

1. Pray for increased insight into how the biblical concept of the priesthood of the believer applies to you personally.

2. Seek courage through prayer to carry out what you believe to be your responsibilities as a believer priest.

3. Pray to be consistent in exercising the opportunities of priesthood, such as a close and direct relationship with God through prayer and worship.

4. Pray that all of the members of your church will embrace the opportunities and responsibilities of being believer priests.

STUDY NOTES

For additional study resources, see www.baptistdistinctives.org

Baptists:
Believer's Baptism

The following activities are based on the Baptist Identity Leaflet No. 8.

Scripture Memory

"Therefore we are buried with him by baptism into death: that like as Christ was raised up from the dead by the glory of the Father, even so we also should walk in newness of life." Romans 6:4

Fill in the Blanks

1. Baptists are one of the very few denominations which practice
_____ _____ by immersion and do so as a
_____ of having been saved, not as a _____ for
salvation.

2. Baptists have been willing to suffer great persecution for their practice of believer's immersion because of _____ _____
_____ based on the Bible.

3. The New Testament records that baptism always _____ conversion, never _____ it, and was not _____ for salvation.

4. Baptism is only for those who have _____ _____ _____
____ _____ _____ ____ _____ _____ _____.

5. Baptists believe that a commitment to believe in and follow Jesus as Lord and Savior is always to be _____.

6. Because of these convictions based on the Bible, Baptists do not baptize _____.

7. Some early Baptists baptized by _____ or _____ _____ over a person, but concluded that baptism by _____ is the biblical way to baptize.

8. The belief in immersion as the proper mode of baptism is based on the Bible for several reasons:

    a. The meaning of the word _____.

    b. The biblical account of Jesus' baptism indicates that it was by _____.

    c. Christ's disciples in _____ _____ times baptized by immersion.

    d. _____ is a means of not only declaring that Christ died, was buried, and was resurrected but also of testifying about our own hope of _____.

    e. The New Testament teaches that immersion is a way to symbolize that __ _____ has died to an old way and is alive to walk in a new way in Christ.

9. There are several examples in the New Testament that demonstrate the belief that baptism is not necessary for salvation: the _____ on the cross, _____ on the Damascus Road, the people in _____ _____, and the persons baptized at _____.

10. Baptism is not a way of _____ saving grace but rather is a way of testifying _____ _____ _____ has been experienced.

11. While baptism is not essential for salvation, it is a very important _____ _____ _____ to the Lord.

12. A reason that Baptists often use the term _____ when referring to baptism is because _____ _____ _____ _____ ___ _____ persons in his name.

13. When possible, a _____ _____ is preferred by Baptists for baptism since baptism is a type of _____ _____ ____ _____ in Christ.

14. Baptism is to follow a person's _____.

15. Baptists regard baptism as a _____ _____.

Application Questions

1. Do you believe that it is essential for a Baptist church to require persons to have experienced biblical baptism by immersion before becoming members? Why or why not?

2. Why do you think that Baptists have been willing to endure persecution by government and religious authorities for practicing baptism by immersion?

3. What do you recall about your own baptism?

4. Since Baptists do not baptize infants, what, if anything, do you believe should be done as a time of dedication of infants?

5. If baptism is an act of obedience to the command of Jesus Christ as Lord, why is it not considered essential to salvation?

6. How close do the baptismal practices of your church come to following the information from the leaflet regarding the person, place, timing, and setting for baptisms?

7. What is meant by, "Baptists regard baptism as a church function"?

8. How soon after a person makes a profession of faith in Christ do you think he or she should be baptized?

9. Who is to decide whether a person has truly been converted and is therefore a proper subject for baptism?

Scripture Application and Memory

Read the scriptures referenced in the leaflet and prayerfully consider how they apply to you. Memorize the passage and its reference in the Scripture Memory section.

> Scripture memory suggestion: **Read** the scripture and reference aloud. **Record** the scripture and reference in your own handwriting. **Review** the scripture word by word. **Reflect** about the meaning and the message it has for you personally. **Recall** the scripture and reference from memory throughout your study time without looking at the scripture.

Suggestions for Prayer

1. Pray for an increased sensitivity to the deep meaning of baptism.

2. Pray for upcoming baptismal services in your church that they will indeed be times of meaningful worship.

3. Pray for persons in the world who are hindered from experiencing believer's baptism because of governmental or other pressures.

4. Thank God for the gift of baptism that symbolizes the death and resurrection of Jesus and of our own death to an old way of life and entering into eternal life with Christ.

STUDY NOTES

For additional study resources, see www.baptistdistinctives.org

Personal Study Guide

Baptists Believe in a Regenerate Church Membership

The following activities are based on the Baptist Identity Leaflet No. 9.

Scripture Memory

"And the Lord added to the church daily such as should be saved." Acts 2:47

Fill in the Blanks

1. Baptists use various terms to describe their _____ of church.

2. Baptists believe that the Bible teaches that _____ persons who have been born again by a _____ _____ of _____ in Christ should be members of a church.

3. Although the New Testament concept of church focuses on a local body of baptized believers in Christ, in a few New Testament passages the word "_____" also refers to the _____ of all the ages.

4. Baptists also believe that saved persons _____ to be members of a church.

5. Although Baptists believe that church membership should include only the redeemed in Christ, they encourage and welcome all persons to _____ _____ activities of the church.

6. Membership in a Baptist church is always to be _____.

7. Baptist churches strive to maintain a born-again membership by the ways they _____ _____ to _____.

8. The vast majority of Baptist churches take very seriously the importance of _____ _____ by immersion prior to church membership.

9. When Baptists vote on a person's request for membership they are not voting on whether the person is _____ or not.

10. One contributing factor to the erosion of the ideal of regenerate church membership seems to be a super-tolerant _____ which prevails in our culture today.

11. The very _____ of our _____ adds to the challenge of maintaining a regenerate church membership.

12. The pressure for _____ _____ of _____ _____ may also be a cause of the erosion of the ideal of a regenerate church membership.

13. The baptism of _____ _____ _____ into membership may also be a cause.

14. In the past many Baptist churches confronted members about _____ that was considered contrary to the Christian life.

15. The apparent decline in a regenerate church membership should be a concern for a _____ of _____.

16. Neglect of such a crucial biblical teaching as regenerate church membership may indicate a lack of commitment to the _____ of the _____.

Application Questions

1. How would you define "regenerate"?

2. What would you say to a person who does not believe in the importance of church membership?

3. What are your church's requirements for church membership?

4. What evidence do you see that indicates a decline in the ideal of a regenerate church membership among Baptists?

5. To what extent do you think the idea of "church discipline" should be renewed in Baptist church life? In your church?

6. What can you do to help achieve a regenerate church membership?

7. What factors in your church may have resulted in an erosion of the ideal of regenerate church membership, if there has been such erosion?

8. What words other than "regenerate" do you believe would communicate the concept?

9. What do you believe are the primary causes for an apparent decline in the proportion of Baptist church members who are born again?

Scripture Application and Memory

Read the scriptures referenced in the leaflet and prayerfully consider how they apply to you. Memorize the passage and its reference in the Scripture Memory section.

> Scripture memory suggestion: **Read** the scripture and reference aloud. **Record** the scripture and reference in your own handwriting. **Review** the scripture word by word. **Reflect** about the meaning and the message it has for you personally. **Recall** the scripture and reference from memory throughout your study time without looking at the scripture.

Suggestions for Prayer

1. Pray for the Holy Spirit to guide you in understanding and applying the truths of the Bible regarding the nature of a church.

2. Pray for your church that it will indeed be composed of persons who have been redeemed.

3. Seek ways through prayer that you can help your church achieve the ideal of a regenerate church membership.

4. Pray for a spirit of concern for persons who present themselves for church membership that they will be given opportunity to understand the nature of salvation and church membership.

5. Pray for ways to emphasize the importance of a regenerate church membership.

STUDY NOTES

Congregational Church Governance

The following activities are based on the Baptist Identity Leaflet No. 10.

Scripture Memory

"So in Christ we who are many form one body, and each member belongs to all the others." Romans 12:5 (NIV)

Fill in the Blanks

1. _____ is how an organization, such as a church, functions.

2. Polity includes the policies that guide matters such as _____, _____ _____, _____, and _____.

3. ____ _____ or _____ outside of any Baptist congregation is to have any authority over the church in regard to beliefs and religious practices.

4. ____ _____ is superior to another in a Baptist church.

5. The reason for this approach to governance is that basic _____ _____ form the foundation for _____ _____.

6. The bases for congregational church governance include the _____ of Christ, the authority of the _____, salvation only by _____ through _____, soul _____ and the priesthood of _____, and _____ _____ _____ of baptized believers.

7. Based on the Bible and major Baptist doctrines, Baptists insist that only _____ is in charge of a church, not any individual or group.

8. _____ and _____ are to be servants and not governors of the church.

9. Baptist polity calls for the _____ _____ to be ultimately responsible for decisions made on the basis of Christ's will for the church.

10. In numbers of churches, the members delegate to _____ and/or _____ the responsibility for certain decisions.

11. Effective congregational church governance depends on the congregation being comprised of persons who are _____ and _____ ____ _____ _____ in Christ.

12. _____ and _____ undermine effective congregational governance.

13. A _____ _____ by a person or group undermines the role of members in decision making in a church.

14. The lack of true congregational governance may be due to the fact that many people simply do not _____ how it functions.

15. The degree to which a church practices congregational governance says a great deal about the _____ _____ of a church.

16. Congregational governance contributes to the development of _____ _____ in the members.

17. Congregational governance is important because it can contribute to the _____ of a church.

18. Congregational governance also is important for _____ ____ _____ and not just for a church.

19. Congregational governance follows the example of the _____ _____ in regard to church governance and is in keeping with _____ _____ _____ that Baptists hold dear.

Application Questions

1. What are some ways to strengthen congregational church governance?

2. What are the needs, if any, in your church to strengthen congregational church governance?

3. In what ways does your church provide every member an opportunity to participate in the governance of your church?

4. Are church business meetings well attended in your church? If not, why do you think this is so? How could attendance be improved?

5. What are some present-day factors in society in general that you believe may affect a change in the approach to church governance away from the New Testament model?

6. In what ways can the practices of church governance demonstrate the basic tenants of our faith?

7. What is the process in your church for making decisions about your church?

8. If congregational governance is being thwarted in your church by individuals or groups, how can you help to correct this?

9. What can be done to improve the knowledge of the reasons for congregational church governance among the members of your church?

10. In a large church, how can a member obtain enough information about the numerous ministries and organizations to be able to help make intelligent decisions?

Scripture Application and Memory

Read the scriptures referenced in the leaflet and prayerfully consider how they apply to you. Memorize the passage and its reference in the Scripture Memory section.

> Scripture memory suggestion: **Read** the scripture and reference aloud. **Record** the scripture and reference in your own handwriting. **Review** the scripture word by word. **Reflect** about the meaning and the message it has for you personally. **Recall** the scripture and reference from memory throughout your study time without looking at the scripture.

Suggestions for Prayer

1. Thank God for the freedom and opportunity of decision-making in your church due to Baptist polity and religious freedom in our country.

2. Pray to be more responsible in being part of the decision process in your church.

3. Pray for help in overcoming any problems to congregational governance in your church.

4. Pray that any person or group attempting to thwart congregational governance in your church will be open to the involvement of all the members in decision making.

5. Pray that persons will realize that Christ is the head of your church and congregational governance is a means of finding and following the will of Christ for your church.

STUDY NOTES

Baptist Autonomy:
Difficulties and Benefits

The following activities are based on the Baptist Identity Leaflet No. 11.

Scripture Memory

"I am Alpha and Omega, the first and the last: and, What thou seest, write in a book, and send it unto the seven churches which are in Asia." Revelation 1:11

Fill in the Blanks

1. Autonomous means _____ or _____.

2. Who is the ultimate authority of a church? _____ _____
_____.

3. Baptists use the term "church" to refer to a _____
_____ and not to the Baptist _____.

4. True or False? There is really no such thing as The Baptist Church. _____

5. Autonomy means that each Baptist church does the following without outside control:

    a. _____ _____ _____ _____.

    b. _____ _____ _____ _____.

    c. _____ _____ _____.

    d. _____ _____ _____ _____
_____.

6. Baptist churches refuse to recognize the authority of governments in matters of:

    a. _____

    b. _____

    c. _____

7. Church autonomy rests on _____ _____ _____.

8. Churches in the New Testament practiced church autonomy in the following ways:

    a. Each church was a _____ _____ under the Lordship of Christ.

    b. Each church resisted the efforts of _____ and _____ _____ to dictate religious beliefs and practices.

9. _____ _____ _____ and the _____ of churches go hand in hand.

10. There are no _____ in the Baptist denomination.

11. Autonomy does not mean _____ of churches from one another or other parts of the denomination.

12. Threats to Baptist autonomy come from _____ the local church and from _____ it.

13. No organization in the Baptist denomination has authority either to _____ or _____ persons who are members of or employed by the churches.

14. Baptists have sought to deal with difficulties related to autonomy through _____ _____.

Application Questions

1. What are some synonyms or other ways to express "autonomy" for Baptist churches?

2. Why is it important that your church remain free from any outside human direction or control in regard to faith and religious practice?

3. What are some appropriate laws for your church to follow?

4. In what ways does the church governance practiced by your church demonstrate church autonomy?

5. Has your church experienced any of the threats to Baptist autonomy mentioned in the leaflet? If so, how can these be countered?

6. What are some reasons that the autonomy of churches is important?

7. What are some of the problems or difficulties a church might face as it remains autonomous? Has your church experienced any of these and if so how has your church dealt with them?

8. What are some examples of the autonomy of local congregations found in the practices of New Testament churches?

9. How can a church remain autonomous and also fulfill the huge responsibilities involved in world missions, ministry to human need, and other issues as directed by the Bible?

Scripture Application and Memory

Read the scriptures referenced in the leaflet and prayerfully consider how they apply to you. Memorize the passage and its reference in the Scripture Memory section.

> Scripture memory suggestion: **Read** the scripture and reference aloud. **Record** the scripture and reference in your own handwriting. **Review** the scripture word by word. **Reflect** about the meaning and the message it has for you personally. **Recall** the scripture and reference from memory throughout your study time without looking at the scripture.

Suggestions for Prayer

1. Pray for sensitivity to anything that might hinder the autonomy of your church.

2. Pray for religious freedom to thrive which enables Baptist autonomy of churches to exist without persecution.

3. Pray for a willingness for more persons to become responsibly involved in the governance of your church.

4. Pray for the leaders of your church as they seek to lead your church to become more and more like the New Testament churches as described in the book of Acts.

STUDY NOTES

Baptist Church Life:
Organization, Officers, Worship, Ordinances

The following activities are based on the Baptist Identity Leaflet No. 12.

Scripture Memory

"...speaking the truth in love, we will in all things grow up into him who is the Head, that is, Christ. From him the whole body, joined and held together by every supporting ligament, grows and builds itself up in love, as each part does its work." Ephesians 4:15-16 (NIV)

Fill in the Blanks

1. _____ and _____, among other things, characterize the life of Baptist churches.

2. This is especially evident with regard to _____, _____, _____, and _____.

3. No entity outside of the church dictates _____ _____ to a Baptist church.

4. The organization of a Baptist church is based on the concept of _____ _____.

5. Since the Bible has little to say about organization of a church, church members have a great deal of freedom as long as the basic _____ _____ purposes of a church are fulfilled.

6. For Baptists the _____ _____ of churches has varied from time to time and place to place.

7. The _____ of a church plays a factor in organization.

8. There is no _____ _____ form of worship for Baptists.

9. In some churches congregational worship is very _____ and _____ while in others it is very _____ and _____.

10. The Bible supports the fact that each church under the leadership of the
_____ ____ _____ ought to be free to determine the
place, elements, and leaders for worship.

11. In order to be genuine, worship must be _____, never _____.

12. The officers in a local New Testament church are _____ and
_____.

13. Baptist churches have used various titles for persons in _____
_____.

14. Each congregation is responsible for the selection of its _____
and _____ according to the biblical requirements for these offices.

15. While important, the role of pastor is not a _____.

16. Baptists do not believe that _____ endows a person
with any special powers or authority.

17. Baptist churches celebrate two ordinances: _____ and _____
_____ _____.

18. The word "ordinances" is used because they were _____ or
_____ by Jesus himself.

19. Baptists contend that baptism and the Lord's Supper, while significant,
are not _____ _____ _____.

20. There is no need for a _____ _____ to administer
either ordinance in a Baptist church.

21. Because baptism and the Lord's Supper are _____, the use
of the proper symbols is important.

22. Using the _____ _____ in the Lord's Supper with a
biblical understanding of them is important.

23. Baptists believe that the elements used in the Supper are not
_____ _____ _____ _____ _____ of Christ but
are _____ of his body and blood.

Application Questions

1. What differences among Baptist churches have you noticed in regard to the worship services and the ordinances?

2. What are some things that allow for these differences in a Baptist church?

3. What improvements, if any, do you think your church should make in regard to the selection and function of a pastor and deacons?

4. What are the policies and procedures followed by your church with regard to ordination?

5. What suggestions would you have for increasing church participation in the observance of church ordinances?

6. What is the symbolism of the two church ordinances?

7. Why do you think that there has been considerable controversy in many Baptist churches over the style of music in worship?

8. Why is it acceptable in a Baptist church for someone other than the pastor to administer the ordinance of baptism?

9. How often do you think the Lord's Supper should be administered?

10. Baptism is considered a one-time experience, but partaking of the Lord's Supper occurs many times in the life of a Christian. Why is this so?

Scripture Application and Memory

Read the scriptures referenced in the leaflet and prayerfully consider how they apply to you. Memorize the passage and its reference in the Scripture Memory section.

> Scripture memory suggestion: **Read** the scripture and reference aloud. **Record** the scripture and reference in your own handwriting. **Review** the scripture word by word. **Reflect** about the meaning and the message it has for you personally. **Recall** the scripture and reference from memory throughout your study time without looking at the scripture.

Suggestions for Prayer

1. Pray for all church members to realize that responsibility is to accompany freedom in church life.

2. Pray for unity in the midst of diversity in your church as well as in the Baptist denomination.

3. Thank God for the diversity and freedom in the Baptist denomination.

4. Pray that no divisive controversy will develop in your church regarding the form and content of worship services.

5. Pray that when the two ordinances are observed, it will be a very worshipful experience for all involved.

STUDY NOTES

Baptists and Voluntary Cooperation

The following activities are based on the Baptist Identity Leaflet No. 13.

Scripture Memory

"Entirely on their own, they urgently pleaded with us for the privilege of sharing in this service to the saints." 2 Corinthians 8:3-4 (NIV)

Fill in the Blanks

1. The Baptist denomination is held together by a rope of sand:
_____   _____.

2. Baptists believe that the Bible teaches that a church should be
_____.

3. Baptists also believe that Christ commanded Christians to be involved in
_____ and _____ throughout the entire world.

4. _____ is a theme that permeates the Baptist symphony of beliefs and polities.

5. The Bible teaches that salvation results only from a _____ faith response to God's grace gift of the Lord Jesus Christ.

6. _____ is a symbol that a person has made a voluntary commitment to Christ as Savior and Lord.

7. A person's decision to become part of a church ought to be
_____.

8. _____   _____ of a Christian ministry should be voluntary.

9. The voluntary nature of churches applies also to the
_____ of _____ to each other and to other parts of the Baptist denomination.

10. The New Testament sets forth the concept of voluntary
_____ among churches.

11. Cooperation among the New Testament churches was for the sake of
_____ _____ to human need, fellowship, missions,
and evangelism.

12. Issues which threatened to divide the early Christian movement were
dealt with through voluntary _____.

13. Another example of voluntary cooperation in the New Testament was
the agreement that certain _____ and _____
would major on different people groups.

14. The New Testament churches in the same _____
_____ had some sort of cooperation with one another.

15. The autonomy obstacle to cooperation among Baptist churches was
cleared by stressing that a church's relationship to any organization beyond
the local church would be _____ _____.

16. Steps toward voluntary cooperation in the Baptist denomination
included the formation of _____ of churches, establishing
organizations termed _____, and the development of
_____.

17. Voluntary cooperation enables churches to do far more together than
they could do alone in such causes as _____, _____,
and _____.

18. Individuals, such as _____ and church staff members, can
benefit from voluntary cooperation.

19. Baptist _____ benefit from voluntary cooperation.

20. _____ and _____ to denominational voluntary
cooperation exist.

21. The challenges to voluntary cooperation can be met by
_____ to objections and _____ its benefits.

22. A _____ of _____ with the strength of _____ describes
Baptist voluntary cooperation.

Application Questions

1. How can your church join with other churches in order to fulfill the global nature of Jesus' command for his disciples?

2. What do you consider to be the strengths and weaknesses of voluntary cooperation?

3. What experiences have you had with various types of voluntary cooperation among Baptist churches?

4. What are the benefits of voluntary cooperation in Baptist life?

5. In what ways has your church benefited from voluntary cooperation?

6. How can a consideration of the five suggestions for dealing with objections given in the leaflet help you with any reservations that you may have regarding the importance of voluntary cooperation?

7. What are some current examples of Baptist "societies" as means of voluntary cooperation?

8. Some Baptists believe that it is unscriptural to have any organizations for Christian ministry other than local churches, such as state conventions, mission boards, and the like. How would you respond to such a concept?

9. What are some examples of voluntary cooperation among Baptist churches in addition to associations and conventions?

Scripture Application and Memory

Read the scriptures referenced in the leaflet and prayerfully consider how they apply to you. Memorize the passage and its reference in the Scripture Memory section.

> Scripture memory suggestion: **Read** the scripture and reference aloud. **Record** the scripture and reference in your own handwriting. **Review** the scripture word by word. **Reflect** about the meaning and the message it has for you personally. **Recall** the scripture and reference from memory throughout your study time without looking at the scripture.

Suggestions for Prayer

1. Pray for persons in your church to be aware of and supportive of efforts of voluntary cooperation within the Baptist denomination.

2. Pray that Baptist individuals and churches will be open to voluntary cooperation in order to reach a lost world.

3. Pray that those Baptist churches which hold to a fierce independence apart from any cooperation will be open to understand the nature and benefit of voluntary cooperation.

4. Pray for efforts to strengthen voluntary cooperation among Baptists throughout the world.

STUDY NOTES

For additional study resources, see www.baptistdistinctives.org

Baptists and Evangelism

The following activities are based on the Baptist Identity Leaflet No. 14.

Scripture Memory

"So then faith cometh by hearing, and hearing by the word of God."
Romans 10:17

Fill in the Blanks

1. Commitment to _____ as a priority is evident in practically every aspect of Baptist life.

2. The Baptist emphasis on evangelism is not based on anything less than the _____ and _____ that comprise Baptist distinctives.

3. Because Jesus is Lord, those who follow him are to do as he _____.

4. For Baptists, the Bible is the authoritative source of teaching about _____ and the _____ _____.

5. Salvation does not come from good works, or through sacraments, or by baptism, or in church membership but only by a _____ _____ to God's grace gift of salvation through Jesus Christ.

6. Baptists believe that the Bible teaches that salvation is _____, that it results from an experience of _____ _____ of sin and faith in Christ.

7. The Bible teaches that the gospel is for _____.

8. Baptists utilize all _____ _____ to urge people to believe in Jesus as Lord and Savior.

9. Baptists believe evangelism is for _____, not just for pastors, missionaries, and evangelists.

10. An individual's sharing the gospel with other people plays a _____ role in evangelism.

11. Evangelism involves sharing the gospel in both _____ and _____.

12. _____ the _____ is another way that Baptists carry out evangelism.

13. _____ by Baptists also carries an evangelistic emphasis.

14. _____ to human need by Baptists also involves a dual purpose—to meet _____, _____, and _____ needs and to share the gospel in order to meet the primary _____ need of salvation in Christ.

15. Baptists provide specific _____ and _____ to encourage and develop evangelism.

16. _____ ought to undergird every aspect of evangelism.

17. _____ and _____ on the part of Christians certainly obstruct effective evangelism.

18. _____, _____, and _____ to embrace the importance of evangelism are also obstacles to evangelism.

19. The Bible teaches both the _____ of God and the _____ of choice of human beings.

20. Baptists are an evangelistic people because of _____ _____ and utilize many means to share the Good News about Jesus Christ.

Application Questions

1. What is your level of commitment to personally sharing the gospel? On what do you base your answer?

2. What would you consider to be some wrong methods of evangelism?

3. How do you relate the sovereignty of God and the freedom of choice of human beings to one another?

4. What are the various methods or approaches to evangelism used by your church? How involved are you in one or more of these?

5. What are the names of at least three persons with whom you can share the gospel?

6. What do you consider to be the greatest obstacle to personal evangelism in your life? In the life of your church?

7. When was the last time that you shared the gospel with another person?

8. Do you agree or disagree with the statement in the opening paragraph of the leaflet which states that "evangelism as a priority is evident in practically every aspect of Baptist life"? What is the basis of your opinion?

9. Do you believe that a commitment to evangelism is increasing or decreasing in the Baptist denomination as a whole? In your church? On what do you base your response?

Scripture Application and Memory

Read the scriptures referenced in the leaflet and prayerfully consider how they apply to you. Memorize the passage and its reference in the Scripture Memory section.

> Scripture memory suggestion: **Read** the scripture and reference aloud. **Record** the scripture and reference in your own handwriting. **Review** the scripture word by word. **Reflect** about the meaning and the message it has for you personally. **Recall** the scripture and reference from memory throughout your study time without looking at the scripture.

Suggestions for Prayer

1. Pray that your own commitment to and involvement in evangelism will be strong.

2. Pray that your church will be effective in evangelistic efforts.

3. Pray for Baptists worldwide that they will be an evangelistic people.

4. Pray for more persons to become involved in evangelistic effort.

5. Pray that specific persons who have not made a faith commitment to Jesus Christ as Lord and Savior will do so.

STUDY NOTES

For additional study resources, see www.baptistdistinctives.org

Baptists and Missions

The following activities are based on the Baptist Identity Leaflet No. 15.

Scripture Memory

"Go ye therefore, and teach all nations, baptizing them in the name of the Father, and of the Son, and of the Holy Ghost: Teaching them to observe all things whatsoever I have commanded you." Matthew 28:19-20

Fill in the Blanks

1. Baptists throughout the world are committed to _____.

2. The word "mission" means ____ ____ _____ to _____ _____ an _____ _____.

3. Being sent by Jesus on mission is part of what it means to _____ _____ as Lord.

4. In the late 1700s, _____ missions began to be a vital part of Baptist life.

5. A number of Baptists, convinced of William Carey's position, joined him in establishing the _____ _____ _____ in the fall of the year _____.

6. As the spirit of missions spread to America, along with Luther Rice, Ann Hasseltine Judson and her husband Adoniram were appointed as _____ _____ to India in the year _____.

7. Careful study of the Bible led the Judsons and Rice to embrace the _____ view.

8. Largely as a result of the efforts of Luther Rice, Baptists formed their first _____ _____ in the United States of America.

9. Baptists continued their efforts in local and nationwide missions but they also began to be a _____ missionary people.

63

10. Most Baptists insist that the _____ _____ make missions mandatory, not optional.

11. The Bible is a _____ _____ and not just a book about missions.

12. The Bible records that the early followers of Christ _____ _____.

13. Mission activity includes _____ _____ and _____ _____ as well as various forms of ministry such as medical, educational, and agricultural.

14. _____ is no longer considered the only organizing principle for missions.

15. One aspect of the international missions involvement is the _____ of Baptist entities in one area with Baptist entities in another in order to expand missions efforts.

16. Baptists _____ missions in various ways.

17. A number of _____ exist for missions today, both internal and external to Baptist life.

Application Questions

1. What evidence is there of your church's response to the Bible's teaching about the importance of missions?

2. What are the mission opportunities that are made available through your church? Local opportunities? Regional? Worldwide?

3. Does your church help to support Baptist missions organizations? Can you describe the activities of these organizations?

4. Do you know the name of at least one family serving in some form of missions service on a full-time basis, such as a career international missionary? If so, do you pray for the family and send words of encouragement to them?

5. What are the most serious challenges to mission activity today?

6. What do you think you could do to help overcome these challenges?

7. With a resurgence of non-Christian religions in various parts of the world, do you believe that Baptists should continue to send missionaries in efforts to share the gospel? Why or why not?

8. Since in some parts of the world for a person to become a Christian is to risk persecution, even death, do you believe we should continue to endeavor to share the gospel there? Why or why not?

9. What does your church do to provide education about missions and to encourage missionary activity? What part do you play in such efforts?

Scripture Application and Memory

Read the scriptures referenced in the leaflet and prayerfully consider how they apply to you. Memorize the passage and its reference in the Scripture Memory section.

> Scripture memory suggestion: **Read** the scripture and reference aloud. **Record** the scripture and reference in your own handwriting. **Review** the scripture word by word. **Reflect** about the meaning and the message it has for you personally. **Recall** the scripture and reference from memory throughout your study time without looking at the scripture.

Suggestions for Prayer

1. Pray for persons to respond to the opportunities and challenges of missionary activity. Jesus taught that his disciples should pray for persons to labor in the "harvest fields."

2. Pray for those persons laboring in dangerous "harvest fields" in various parts of the world.

3. Pray for your church to be indeed a church involved in all aspects of missions.

4. Pray for the obstacles and challenges to mission endeavors to be overcome.

STUDY NOTES

For additional study resources, see www.baptistdistinctives.org

Baptists and Ministry

The following activities are based on the Baptist Identity Leaflet No. 16.

Scripture Memory

"Inasmuch as ye have done it unto one of the least of these my brethren, ye have done it unto me." Matthew 25:40

Fill in the Blanks

1. One of the ways that Baptists strive to live out their faith is by _____ to the total needs of people.

2. Baptist ministry to people is rooted in _____ _____ _____ and _____.

3. Jesus set an example in his ministry of caring for all people and for their total needs — _____, _____, _____, _____, and _____.

4. Jesus as Lord taught the _____ of ministry.

5. The _____ makes clear the importance of _____ to total human need.

6. Individuals who are saved by faith in Jesus Christ as Lord and Savior become _____ _____.

7. Baptist ministry is rooted in _____ participation, support, and cooperation.

8. The extent of Baptist ministry is based on the _____ and _____ of Jesus and the _____ of the Bible.

9. Ministry is for the _____ person, for all kinds of _____, and in all sorts of _____.

10. Baptist ministry is delivered by an extensive array of _____.

11. Dedicated individuals make up the corps of _____
and staff members who enable churches and other organizations to minister
to people.

12. _____ _____ of various sizes and locations
minister to human need.

13. _____ _____ including schools, children's
homes, and medical centers minister to human need.

14. _____ _____ of different kinds meet
the needs of persons in numerous ways.

15. _____ _____, _____,
_____, and _____ of churches
foster many of these institutions and organizations of ministry.

16. Ministry in _____ _____ plays a major role in Baptist life.

17. Instructed by the _____ and empowered by the _____
_____, Baptists endeavor to minister in Jesus' name to the total
person, to all people, and in all places to the glory of God the Father.

Application Questions

1. What are some of the opportunities that are made available through your church to minister to the needs of persons?

2. Based on the importance of ministry in the life of Jesus, what specific actions do you believe that your church should take to meet human need?

3. What experiences have you had personally encountering someone in need of ministry?

4. What suggestions would you make to help maintain the proper balance between meeting needs other than spiritual needs with the importance of always addressing a person's spiritual needs?

5. What are some of the obstacles or challenges of ministering to needs that you have experienced? How can these be overcome?

6. How many specific ministries to human need sponsored by Baptist conventions are you aware of? Is your church involved in assisting with these?

7. How effective is the ministry to needs of church members through your Sunday School or deacon ministry? How can you strengthen your participation in these ministries?

8. What specific ministries does your church have to meet physical need? Emotional need? Social need? Spiritual need?

Scripture Application and Memory

Read the scriptures referenced in the leaflet and prayerfully consider how they apply to you. Memorize the passage and its reference in the Scripture Memory section.

> Scripture memory suggestion: **Read** the scripture and reference aloud. **Record** the scripture and reference in your own handwriting. **Review** the scripture word by word. **Reflect** about the meaning and the message it has for you personally. **Recall** the scripture and reference from memory throughout your study time without looking at the scripture.

Suggestions for Prayer

1. Pray for the persons in your church who are ministering in the name of Jesus to human need.

2. Pray for the various Baptist individuals and institutions ministering in the name of Jesus to those in need.

3. Pray for a sensitivity to the needs of persons and how you can best help meet those needs.

4. Pray that Baptist efforts to meet human need will focus always on both the physical and the spiritual needs of persons.

STUDY NOTES

Baptists and Christian Education

The following activities are based on the Baptist Identity Leaflet No. 17.

Scripture Memory

"The fear of the Lord is the beginning of knowledge: but fools despise wisdom and instruction." Proverbs 1:7

Fill in the Blanks

1. Baptists believe in making _____ _____ available for all persons and deliver it in a multitude of ways.

2. The commitment to Christian education rests solidly on the _____ of the _____.

3. The Bible stresses the importance of enriching the _____ as well as the _____.

4. The knowledge of God is best found in the _____.

5. Christian education appropriately includes study of the _____ _____ as well as _____ _____.

6. Baptists also provide Christian education because they believe that it helps to make strong and effective _____ and contributes to a just and stable _____ _____.

7. Baptist _____ and _____ lead to the Baptist commitment to Christian education.

8. The Baptist belief in _____ _____ and the _____ of all believers calls for Christian education.

9. _____ _____ and local church _____, both Baptist polities, are strengthened by Christian education.

10. _____, _____, _____, and the application of the gospel to daily life are all made more effective by Christian education.

11. _____ _____ is secured and advanced by people who are well-grounded through Christian education in the _____ and in _____.

12. Baptists make available _____ for many kinds of Christian education, _____ and _____.

13. Baptists believe that education is for _____ _____.

14. Some teaching and training is provided by Baptists primarily for _____ _____ _____ as well as for _____.

15. Baptists use a variety of _____ and delivery systems to provide Christian education, such as _____, associations of churches, _____, and various _____ and organizations.

16. Baptists deal with a number of _____ related to Christian education.

17. At _____ _____ Baptists have provided a wide variety of educational opportunities for Baptists and others.

Application Questions

1. What experiences have you had personally with the provision made by Baptists in the area of Christian education?

2. In what ways has this study strengthened your commitment to the importance of participating through your church toward the support of Christian education opportunities?

3. How are religious freedom and Christian education related?

4. Can you name at least five Baptist universities?

5. How important to you is the idea of Christian education for laypersons and not just for those who are preparing for or are in some vocational church position, such as a pastor?

6. What are the various opportunities for Christian education that are made available in your church? Which ones of these are you involved in?

7. Which challenges to Christian education are the most serious?

8. How are you helping to overcome the challenges to Christian education? In your church? In the Baptist denomination?

9. Why do you think some people consider Baptists to be anti-education? What are some ways to counter this impression?

Scripture Application and Memory

Read the scriptures referenced in the leaflet and prayerfully consider how they apply to you. Memorize the passage and its reference in the Scripture Memory section.

> Scripture memory suggestion: **Read** the scripture and reference aloud. **Record** the scripture and reference in your own handwriting. **Review** the scripture word by word. **Reflect** about the meaning and the message it has for you personally. **Recall** the scripture and reference from memory throughout your study time without looking at the scripture.

Suggestions for Prayer

1. Pray that those who lead Baptist schools, such as presidents and other administrators, will be able to overcome the challenges faced by them.

2. Pray for those who teach in various positions in Baptist life to be effective in this very important ministry.

3. Pray for the various aspects of your church's program of Christian education.

4. Thank God for giving guidance and encouragement to Baptists who pioneered in Christian education, often at great sacrifice.

5. Pray that Baptist beliefs and polity will be strengthened by your involvement in and support of Christian education.

STUDY NOTES

For additional study resources, see www.baptistdistinctives.org

Baptists:
Applying the Gospel

The following activities are based on the Baptist Identity Leaflet No. 18.

Scripture Memory

"...And what does the Lord require of you? To act justly and to love mercy and to walk humbly with your God." Micah 6:8 (NIV)

Fill in the Blanks

1. Baptists declare that Christians have a responsibility both to _____ the gospel and to _____ it to all of life.

2. The application of the principles of Christianity to social conditions calls for both _____ and _____ _____.

3. Ministry involves efforts to heal the hurts of people including _____, _____, _____, and _____.

4. Social action involves efforts to change the _____ which cause hurts.

5. Baptists' efforts to right the wrongs in our world are based solidly on bedrock Baptist beliefs such as _____ _____ ____ _____ and _____ _____ ____ _____ _____.

6. The Lordship of Christ calls for efforts to bring about a social order characterized by _____ and _____.

7. Jesus declared that the Great Commandment is to love _____ and _____.

8. Jesus publicly announced his ministry in terms that indicated his concern for _____ _____ ____ _____.

9. Jesus set an example of _____ _____ for the benefit of others.

10. Jesus addressed specific issues related to institutions of society, such as _____ and _____.

11. The _____ _____ records God's will for the institutions of society.

12. The _____ _____ records that the Christians in the earliest churches stressed God's will for a just, humane, and moral social order.

13. _____ _____ strengthen the social order by living in accord with the teachings of the Bible in daily life.

14. Baptist _____, _____ of churches, _____, and _____ through various organized efforts strive to develop a more just and humane social order.

15. Baptists believe that _____ _____ coupled with _____ will bring about positive social change.

16. Baptists preach, teach, and write to set forth standards of the Bible for the _____ _____.

17. Efforts to apply the gospel to the social order meet many _____.

18. Applying the gospel is also difficult because quite often there is _____ ____ _____ as to which problems should be confronted.

19. Some people question the _____ of efforts to correct ills in society.

20. _____ and _____ play a huge role in thwarting effective efforts to apply the gospel.

Application Questions

1. How effective would you consider yourself to be at applying the principles of Christianity to the social conditions in your area? How effective is your church in doing this?

2. Do you find it easier to participate in actions of ministry or of social action? Why?

3. What do you believe that Baptists are more effective in doing—ministry or social action? Why?

4. What is your response to the idea that bearing one's cross includes participation in social action?

5. What are some ways that you would suggest to help your church combine evangelism and social action?

6. What is your opinion of the idea that Christians may have to become involved in boycotts and public demonstrations for the sake of social reform?

7. How can a church impact politics without becoming political?

8. In your opinion what are the most damaging conditions in our society?

Scripture Application and Memory

Read the scriptures referenced in the leaflet and prayerfully consider how they apply to you. Memorize the passage and its reference in the Scripture Memory section.

> Scripture memory suggestion: **Read** the scripture and reference aloud. **Record** the scripture and reference in your own handwriting. **Review** the scripture word by word. **Reflect** about the meaning and the message it has for you personally. **Recall** the scripture and reference from memory throughout your study time without looking at the scripture.

Suggestions for Prayer

1. Pray for an increased awareness of the needs of persons who live in your community.

2. Pray for insight and courage to help bring about a more loving and just social order.

3. Pray for those who are leading efforts for social change in keeping with the teachings of the Bible.

4. Pray that your church will become increasingly involved in both ministry and social action.

STUDY NOTES

For additional study resources, see www.baptistdistinctives.org

Baptists
Champions of Religious Freedom

The following activities are based on the Baptist Identity Leaflet No. 19.

Scripture Memory

"...ye have been called unto liberty; only use not liberty for an occasion to the flesh, but by love serve one another." Galatians 5:13

Fill in the Blanks

1. The Baptist devotion to religious freedom is closely related to other biblical truths that comprise the Baptist mosaic of _____ and _____.

2. The bases for religious freedom include the belief in the freedom to _____ and _____ the _____.

3. In the earliest days of the Christian movement government officials _____ _____ _____.

4. The use of the power of the state to enforce religion sapped the _____ _____ of the established state churches and added a host of _____ people to the churches.

5. _____ suffered severely under the union of _____ and _____.

6. Early Baptists in America believed that the only way full religious freedom could be achieved was through a friendly _____ of church and state.

7. The record of the Baptist struggle for _____ _____ and the separation of church and state is a story of _____ and _____.

8. A host of brave people stayed with their convictions in the face of stiff resistance from both _____ and _____ authorities.

9. Leaders in the Baptist effort for religious freedom for all persons included Thomas _____, John _____, Roger _____, Isaac _____, and John _____.

10. John Leland reportedly met with _____ _____ to encourage his efforts for the inclusion of religious liberty in the Constitution of the United States.

11. The Constitution of the United States, at first flawed by its lack of guarantee of religious freedom, was amended under _____ leadership to provide such a guarantee.

12. Baptists of today should do at least the following to protect and advance the precious heritage of religious freedom: _____ the religious freedom that we enjoy in our nation; _____ religious freedom; _____ _____ for religious freedom throughout the world; _____ the friendly separation of church and state; _____ _____ with religious freedom; _____ _____ for the benefit of others.

13. At great peril and huge sacrifice Baptists helped to provide religious freedom for multitudes in this generation. Now it is up to the _____ of _____ to help preserve this precious heritage for the generations to follow.

Application Questions

1. Why is it important to emphasize the *friendly* separation of church and state in regard to providing religious freedom for all persons?

2. What are some examples of ways that certain groups or individuals attempt to deny religious freedom in our day?

3. What is the best way to demonstrate appreciation for those who have made great sacrifices for the sake of the religious freedom that we enjoy?

4. Which issues regarding the separation of church and state give you the greatest concern?

5. What are some ways that your church can help members to gain a new appreciation for the importance of religious freedom?

6. What are some ways that your church can help members understand how to preserve and protect religious freedom?

7. How does religious freedom benefit you? How can you use religious freedom to benefit others?

8. Since some religions do not believe in religious freedom but rather believe in a relation of religious organizations and the government where a particular religion is enforced/supported by the government, do you think it is right for Baptists to attempt to gain religious freedom for all persons everywhere? Why?

Scripture Application and Memory

Read the scriptures referenced in the leaflet and prayerfully consider how they apply to you. Memorize the passage and its reference in the Scripture Memory section.

> Scripture memory suggestion: **Read** the scripture and reference aloud. **Record** the scripture and reference in your own handwriting. **Review** the scripture word by word. **Reflect** about the meaning and the message it has for you personally. **Recall** the scripture and reference from memory throughout your study time without looking at the scripture.

Suggestions for Prayer

1. Thank God for the emphasis in the Bible on the importance of religious freedom.

2. Pray for religious and government leaders in our nation to strive to preserve religious freedom for all.

3. Pray for those persons who live in places where there is little or no religious freedom as they practice their Christian faith at great peril.

4. Pray that our government will not grow slack in working for religious freedom around the world.

STUDY NOTES

For additional study resources, see www.baptistdistinctives.org

Answers to the Fill in the Blanks

Leaflet No. 1 — Baptists: Who? Where? What? Why?
1. (misunderstood) 2. (beliefs) (practices) (heritage) (history) 3. (group) (of) (beliefs) (and) (practices) 4. a. (Racially) b. (Economically) c. (Politically) d. (Educationally) e. (Religiously) f. (Culturally) 5. (hundred) (countries) 6. (50) (million) 7. (North) (America) 8. (Europe) (North) (America) 9. (evangelism) (missions) 10. (human) (hurt) 11. (Lordship) (Bible) (soul) (competency) (voluntary) (priesthood) (believers) (immersion) (regenerate) 12. (church) (governance) (autonomy) (baptism) (Lord's) (Supper) (tithes) (offerings) (worship) (styles) 13. (evangelism) (missions) (ministry) (gospel) (Christian) (education) 14. (Voluntarism) 15. (basic) (beliefs) (practices)

Leaflet No. 2 — Baptists: What Makes a Baptist a Baptist?
1. (denomination) (religious) (organization) 2. (beliefs) (practices) 3. (organizations) 4. (church) (salvation) (baptism) 5. (persons) (world) 6. (True) 7. (beliefs) (practices) 8. (certain) (ingredients) 9. (other) (denominations) 10. (True) 11. (George) (W.) (Truett) 12. (distinctive) (beliefs) (Baptist) (denomination) 13. (Baptist) (denomination) 14. (belief) (in) (God) (Jesus) (Christ) 15. (baptism) (human) (founder) 16. (voluntary) (cooperation) 17. (New) (Testament)

Leaflet No. 3 — Jesus Is Lord
1. (total) (allegiance) (loving) (service) (faithful) (obedience) (is) (done) 2. (divine) (died) (rose) (ascended) 3. (the) (Lordship) (of) (Christ) (Bible) 4. (soul) (competency) (God) 5. (the) (Lordship) (of) (Christ) 6. (the) (head) (of) (the) (church) 7. (creation) (person) (churches) 8. (direct) 9. (freedom) (responsibility) (of) (choices) 10. (competence) (responsibility) 11. (government) (religious) (organizations) 12. (King) (James) 13. (Lord) (all) 14. (Christian) (doctrine)

Leaflet No. 4 — The Authority of the Bible
1. (nature) 2. (uniquely) (from) (God) (God) 3. a. (unity) b. (Old) (Testament) (prophecies) c. (relevance) d. (power) (transform) e. (claims) 4. (authoritative) 5. (Bible) (God) 6. (written) (ultimate) 7. (revelation) 8. (Lordship) (authority) 9. (enlightens) (illumines) 10. (religion) 11. (Baptist) (doctrine) (church) (polity) 12. (possess) (read) (interpret) 13. a. (guidance) b. (believers) c. (principles) d. (mature) (Christians) 14. (Bible) (sole) (ultimate) (written) (authority)

Leaflet No. 5 — Is Soul Competency *THE* Baptist Distinctive?
1. (gift) (from) (God) 2. (to) (make) (choices) 3. (soul) (competency) 4. (Ten) (Commandments) 5. (choices) (to) (make) (decisions) 6. (Elijah) (Jeremiah) (Isaiah) 7. (coerced) 8. (soul) (freedom) 9. (Church) (leaders) 10. (God's) (sovereignty) 11. (human) (arrogance) (pride) 12. (subjectivism) 13. (foundational) 14. (authority) (Bible) (salvation) (religious) (freedom) (priesthood) (believer's) (baptism) 15. (despise) (freedom) 16. (responsibility)

Leaflet No. 6 — Baptists: Salvation By Grace Through Faith Alone
1. (sinned) (eternal) (death) 2. (sin) (hell) (heaven) (faith) 3. (grace) (faith) (works) 4. (salvation) 5. (faith) 6. (baptism) (church) (membership) (good) (works) (sacraments) 7. (faith) (grace) (gift) 8. (cost) 9. (lightly) 10. (regeneration) (sanctification) (glorification) 11. (Good) (works) (good) (works) 12. (coerced) 13. (compelled) 14. (freedom) (of) (choice) 15. (relationship) (free) (will) 16. (sovereignty) (freedom) (of) (choice) 17. (repentance) (and) (faith) (saved) 18. (security) (of) (the) (believer)

Leaflet No. 7 — Baptists: The Priesthood of the *Believer* or of *Believers*?
1. (priests) (believer) (priests) 2. (opportunity) (responsibility) 3. (High) (Priest) 4. (priests) (human) (mediators) 5. (share) (word) (deed) 6. (evangelism) (missions) (ministry) (social) (action) 7. (Martin) (Luther) 8. (pastors) 9. (New) (Testament) 10. (soul) (competency) 11. (read) (interpret) (Bible) 12. (Jesus) (Christ) 13. (priests) 14. (believers) 15. (fellowship) 16. (believer) (priests) 17. (church) 18. (prayer) (Bible) (study) (meditation) (discussion) 19. (the) (priesthood) (of) (the) (believer) (priesthood) (of) (believers) 20. (individual) (group)

Answers to the Fill in the Blanks (cont.)

Leaflet No. 8 — Baptists: Believer's Baptism
1. (believer's) (baptism) (symbol) (requirement) 2. (basic) (Baptist) (convictions) 3. (followed) (preceded) (necessary) 4. (put) (their) (faith) (in) (Jesus) (Christ) (as) (Lord) (and) (Savior) 5. (voluntary) 6. (infants) 7. (pouring) (sprinkling) (water) (immersion) 8. a. (baptize) b. (immersion) c. (New) (Testament) d. (Immersion) (resurrection) e. (a) (believer) 9. (thief) (Saul) (Cornelius') (house) (Pentecost) 10. (channeling) (that) (saving) (grace) 11. (ingredient) (for) (obedience) 12. (ordinance) (Jesus) (ordered) (his) (disciples) (to) (baptize) 13. (public) (place) (public) (profession) (of) (faith) 14. (conversion) 15. (church) (function)

Leaflet No. 9 — Baptists Believe in a Regenerate Church Membership
1. (concept) 2. (only) (genuine) (experience) (faith) 3. (church) (redeemed) 4. (ought) 5. (attend) (various) 6. (voluntary) 7. (admit) (persons) (membership) 8. (believer's) (baptism) 9. (saved) 10. (attitude) 11. (nature) (society) 12. (increased) (size) (church) (membership) 13. (very) (young) (children) 14. (behavior) 15. (number) (reasons) 16. (authority) (Bible)

Leaflet No. 10 — Congregational Church Governance
1. (Polity) 2. (governance) (decision) (making) (structure) (leadership) 3. (No) (person) (group) 4. (No) (individual) 5. (Baptist) (beliefs) (congregational) (governance) 6. (Lordship) (Bible) (grace) (faith) (competency) (believers) (regenerate) (church) (membership) 7. (Christ) 8. (Pastors) (deacons) 9. (entire) (membership) 10. (committees) (staff) 11. (redeemed) (growing) (to) (healthy) (maturity) 12. (Apathy) (indifference) 13. (dictatorial) (spirit) 14. (understand) 15. (basic) (beliefs) 16. (Christian) (maturity) 17. (vitality) 18. (society) (in) (general) 19. (New) (Testament) (basic) (biblical) (doctrines)

Leaflet No. 11 — Baptist Autonomy: Difficulties and Benefits
1. (self-governing) (self-directing) 2. (Jesus) (as) (Lord) 3. (local) (congregation) (denomination) 4. (True) 5. a. (Selects) (its) (pastoral) (leadership) b. (Determines) (its) (worship) (form) c. (Decides) (financial) (matters) d. (Directs) (other) (church) (related) (affairs) 6. a. (doctrine) b. (polity) c. (ministry) 7. (basic) (Baptist) (convictions) 8. a. (separate) (entity) b. (governmental) (religious) (authorities) 9. (Congregational) (church) (governance) (autonomy) 10. (levels) 11. (isolation) 12. (outside) (inside) 13. (discipline) (protect) 14. (voluntary) (cooperation)

Leaflet No. 12 — Baptist Church Life
1. (Freedom) (variety) 2. (organization) (worship) (officers) (ordinances) 3. (organizational) (structure) 4. (congregational) (governance) 5. (New) (Testament) 6. (organizational) (structure) 7. (size) 8. (prescribed) (denominational) 9. (structured) (formal) (unstructured) (informal) 10. (Lordship) (of) (Christ) 11. (free) (coerced) 12. (pastor) (deacon) 13. (pastoral) (leadership) 14. (pastor) (deacons) 15. (dictatorship) 16. (ordination) 17. (baptism) (the) (Lord's) (Supper) 18. (ordered) (commanded) 19. (necessary) (for) (salvation) 20. (priestly) (class) 21. (symbolic) 22. (correct) (elements) 23. (literally) (the) (body) (and) (blood) (symbols)

Leaflet No. 13 — Baptists and Voluntary Cooperation
1. (voluntary) (cooperation) 2. (autonomous) 3. (missions) (ministry) 4. (Voluntarism) 5. (voluntary) 6. (Baptism) 7. (voluntary) 8. (Financial) (support) 9. (relationship) (congregations) 10. (cooperation) 11. (effective) (ministry) 12. (cooperation) 13. (evangelists) (missionaries) 14. (geographical) (region) 15. (purely) (voluntary) 16. (associations) (societies) (conventions) 17. (missions) (ministry) (education) 18. (pastors) 19. (institutions) 20. (Obstacles) (challenges) 21. (responding) (explaining) 22. (rope) (sand) (steel)

Answers to the Fill in the Blanks (cont.)

Leaflet No. 14 — Baptists and Evangelism
1. (evangelism) 2. (beliefs) (practices) 3. (commands) 4. (doctrine) (Christian) (life) 5. (faith) (response) 6. (experiential) (personal) (repentance) 7. (everyone) 8. (legitimate) (means) 9. (everyone) 10. (vital) 11. (deeds) (words) 12. (Preaching) (gospel) 13. (Teaching) 14. (Ministry) (physical) (mental) (emotional) (spiritual) 15. (organizations) (meetings) 16. (Prayer) 17. (Apathy) (indifference) 18. (Fear) (doubt) (failure) 19. (sovereignty) (freedom) 20. (basic) (beliefs)

Leaflet No. 15 — Baptists and Missions
1. (missions) 2. (to) (be) (sent) (carry) (out) (assigned) (task) 3. (follow) (him) 4. (worldwide) 5. (Baptist) (Missionary) (Society) (1792) 6. (Congregational) (missionaries) (1812) 7. (Baptist) 8. (national) (organization) 9. (worldwide) 10. (Bible's) (teachings) 11. (missionary) (book) 12. (affirmed) (missions) 13. (personal) (witnessing) (church) (starting) 14. (Geography) 15. (partnering) 16. (support) 17. (challenges)

Leaflet No. 16 — Baptists and Ministry
1. (ministering) 2. (basic) (Baptist) (beliefs) (polity) 3. (physical) (emotional) (mental) (social) (spiritual) 4. (importance) 5. (Bible) (ministry) 6. (believer) (priests) 7. (voluntary) 8. (example) (teachings) (instructions) 9. (total) (people) (places) 10. (methods) 11. (volunteers) 12. (Baptist) (churches) 13. (Baptist) (institutions) 14. (Baptist) (organizations) 15. (Baptist) (conventions) (unions) (associations) (networks) 16. (numerous) (forms) 17. (Bible) (Holy) (Spirit)

Leaflet No. 17 — Baptists and Christian Education
1. (Christian) (education) 2. (teachings) (Bible) 3. (mind) (spirit) 4. (Bible) 5. (physical) (world) (theological) (reflection) 6. (churches) (social) (order) 7. (beliefs) (polity) 8. (soul) (competency) (priesthood) 9. (Congregational) (governance) (autonomy) 10. (Evangelism) (missions) (ministry) 11. (Religious) (freedom) (Bible) (history) 12. (resources) (formal) (informal) 13. (all) (persons) 14. (vocational) (church) (leadership) (laypersons) 15. (methods) (churches) (conventions) (institutions) 16. (challenges) 17. (considerable) (sacrifice)

Leaflet No. 18 — Baptists: Applying the Gospel
1. (share) (apply) 2. (ministry) (social) (action) 3. (spiritual) (physical) (mental) (emotional) 4. (circumstances) 5. (the) (Lordship) (of) (Christ) (the) (authority) (of) (the) (Bible) 6. (love) (justice) 7. (God) (others) 8. (all) (aspects) (of) (life) 9. (sacrificial) (service) 10. (family) (government) 11. (Old) (Testament) 12. (New) (Testament) 13. (Baptist) (individuals) 14. (churches) (associations) (networks) (conventions) 15. (authentic) (evangelism) (discipleship) 16. (social) (order) 17. (challenges) 18. (lack) (of) (agreement) 19. (validity) 20. (Apathy) (indifference)

Leaflet No. 19 — Baptists: Champions of Religious Freedom
1. (beliefs) (practices) 2. (read) (interpret) (Bible) 3. (severely) (persecuted) (Christians) 4. (spiritual) (vitality) (unsaved) 5. (Baptists) (church) (state) 6. (separation) 7. (religious) (freedom) (courage) (persistence) 8. (religious) (government) 9. (Helwys) (Bunyan) (Williams) (Backus) (Leland) 10. (James) (Madison) 11. (Madison's) 12. (appreciate) (guard) (support) (efforts) (uphold) (act) (responsibly) (use) (freedom) 13. (Baptists) (today)

About the *Baptist Identity Series*

Concern! Vision! Action! Cooperation! Results!
These words describe how the *Baptist Identity Series* came about.

Concern. A dedicated Baptist layman and active churchman, Noble Hurley, became quite concerned about the diminishing understanding by Baptists and others of basic Baptist beliefs and practices. Aware of the contributions by Baptists to the mission of the Lord Jesus Christ, he was concerned that a lack of knowledge about and commitment to Baptist beliefs would lead to erosion of the Baptist contributions to the cause of Christ and to the world in general. He was not alone in his concern.

Vision. A person of vision, Hurley believed that widespread informative and inspirational materials about Baptists as related to biblical truth could be used to increase understanding of what Baptists believe and practice.

Action. He acted to make such materials a reality. He realized that Baptists hold no monopoly on truth and did not want to disparage any other denomination. However, he wanted to perpetuate the Baptist beliefs and practices which had benefited multitudes of persons through centuries. To this end he asked William M. Pinson, Jr. and Doris A. Tinker to prepare the materials and provided funds to publish the materials.

Cooperation. As work began on the preparation of materials on Baptist identity, many persons, including pastors, historians, theologians, and Sunday School teachers, were enlisted to assist in a variety of ways. The materials first appeared as colorful articles in the *Baptist Standard.* A website was developed for the articles, resources, and other information. The positive response to the articles led to the development of the *Baptist Identity Series* that was made possible by the cooperative efforts of many.

Results. The many requests for the articles to be available in leaflet form led to the development of nineteen Baptist Identity Leaflets in a colorful 4-page 5.5 x 8.5 format. In order to enhance the usefulness of the leaflets, a book of nineteen study guides was prepared for use by persons in individual study and/or group study of the leaflets. Also, a book was developed for persons leading group studies containing study guides on the nineteen leaflets along with suggestions for leading the studies. Requests for the leaflets to also be available in a book led to the development of *Baptist Beliefs and Heritage,* an 11 x 8.5 volume that contains the nineteen Baptist Identity Leaflets, a summary of Baptist history, biographical sketches of Baptist leaders, insights on key words and terms used in the materials, historical vignettes, and brief accounts of persons and events in Baptist heritage. Thus the *Baptist Identity Series* consists of these items: three books—*Personal Study Guides, Leader's Guide for Group Study,* and *Baptist Beliefs and Heritage*—and nineteen individual Baptist Identity Leaflets.

Contributors to the *Baptist Identity Series*

Material Preparation
Many persons cooperated in the development of the materials of the *Baptist Identity Series*. The following were the primary contributors:

William M. Pinson, Jr. authored the materials in the *Baptist Identity Series*. He has served as a seminary professor, pastor, interim pastor in Texas, Kansas, and New York, president of Golden Gate Baptist Seminary in California, executive director of the Baptist General Convention of Texas (BGCT), and member of various commissions of the Baptist World Alliance. He has taught and written extensively on Baptists.

Doris A. Tinker served as the primary designer for the *Series* leaflets and books, assisted in research and editing, and coordinated the entire project. She has served as a volunteer in Baptist churches in Arkansas, Illinois, and Texas, pastor's secretary, long-time executive associate in the BGCT executive director's office, communications/organization director of the Texas Baptist Heritage Center, and facilitator for many meetings on Baptist identity.

Dennis A. Parrott provided valuable input for the personal and group study guides. He has served as minister of education in a number of Baptist churches and as the director of the Bible study department of the BGCT. He has authored curriculum material for various Baptist publications.

Skyler G. Tinker assisted in developing the graphics and layout for the leaflets and the study guides. He comes from a deep Baptist background and has been part of a Baptist church all of his life. He graduated from the University of Texas at Dallas majoring in arts and technology with a minor in computer science.

Others, such as the following, contributed in various ways. Stephanie and Aaron Beazley, each a part of generations of strong Baptist families, assisted in editing materials and preparing them for printing and also contributed to updating the website on Baptist distinctives www.baptistdistinctives.org. Debbie O'Toole, Sunday School teacher and Baptist pastor's daughter, provided consultation as representative of the company that printed the *Series*. Looie Biffar, long-time Baptist denominational worker, provided technical assistance.

Financial Assistance
A number of individuals and entities, including the following, embraced the vision of the *Baptist Identity Series* and contributed financially, making the materials available at very reasonable costs: The Jane and Noble Hurley Baptist Identity Fund, Bill and Ruth Landes Pitts through the James and Irene Landes Memorial Fund, Vester T. Hughes, Jr., and The Prichard Family Foundation.

How to Order Materials
in the
Baptist Identity Series

For current information on ordering, including price and shipping information, see the website www.baptistdistinctives.org.

The *Baptist Identity Series* is made up of the following items:

1. ***Baptist Beliefs and Heritage***—an 11 x 8.5 book that contains the Baptist Identity Leaflets,* a summary of Baptist history, biographical sketches of Baptist leaders, insights on key words and terms in the *Series,* historical vignettes, and pertinent information on each of the nineteen leaflets related to Baptist heritage.

   * Baptist Identity Leaflets—a set of nineteen colorful leaflets in a 4-page 5.5 x 8.5 format on Baptist beliefs and practices on which the study guides are based. As indicated above they are in the bound copy of the *Baptist Beliefs and Heritage* book. They are also available in a packet containing all nineteen leaflets.

2. ***Personal Study Guides***—a 5.5 x 8.5 book containing nineteen guides for use by persons in individual or group study on the topics in the Baptist Identity Leaflets.

3. ***Leader's Guide for Group Study***—a 5.5 x 8.5 book for leaders of study groups containing guides for each of the leaflets on the topics in the Baptist Identity Leaflets.

The following information may be helpful in ordering:

The ***Baptist Beliefs and Heritage*** book is helpful for anyone wishing to learn about Baptist identity. It is especially designed for use by persons studying the Baptist Identity Leaflets either as an individual or as part of a group. The book would be an ideal gift to a new church member or to someone interested in becoming a member of a Baptist church.

The ***Personal Study Guides*** book is a companion to the *Baptist Beliefs and Heritage* book. It is designed with learning activities for persons in studying the Baptist Identity Leaflets either as an individual or as part of a group.

The ***Leader's Guide for Group Study*** book is designed for persons who are leading groups in studying the Baptist Identity Leaflets or who are considering establishing or leading such groups. It contains suggested teaching guides for each of the nineteen leaflets. A person leading such a group as well as the members of the group will need to have both the *Baptist Beliefs and Heritage* book and the *Personal Study Guides* book.

The ***Baptist Identity Leaflets*** in the separate leaflet format can be used in a variety of ways, such as handouts in worship services or other meetings, resources for special events including baptismal services and the Lord's Supper, or as gifts to persons interested in knowing about Baptist beliefs.